IN THE NEWS Need to Know

Censorship

by Ashley Kuehl

Consultant: Caitlin Krieck, Social Studies Teacher and Instructional Coach, The Lab School of Washington

Minneapolis, Minnesota

Credits

Cover and title page, © Jacob Lund/Shutterstock; 5, © fizkes/Shutterstock; 7, © Yevhen/Adobe Stock and © BORT GRAPHIC/Adobe Stock and © photoguns/Adobe Stock; 9, © Richard Levine/Alamy Stock Photo; 11, © Monkey Business Images/Adobe Stock; 13, © Wavebreakmedia/iStock; 15, © Halfpoint/Adobe Stock; 17, © MARK SAMPSON/Adobe Stock; 19T, © Bettmann Archive/Getty Images; 19B, © Star Tribune /Getty Images; 21, © Bettmann Archive/Getty Images; 23, © CarlosBarquero/Adobe Stock; 25, © Ryan Collerd/AP Images; 27, © monkeybusinessimages/iStock; 28TL, © " Ali Cotterill"/Wikimedia; 28ML, © David Eggert/AP Images; 28BL, © Emily Tirella Photography, 2018

Bearport Publishing Company Product Development Team

Publisher: Jen Jenson; Director of Product Development: Spencer Brinker; Managing Editor: Allison Juda; Editor: Cole Nelson; Associate Editor: Naomi Reich; Associate Editor: Tiana Tran; Art Director: Colin O'Dea; Designer: Kim Jones; Designer: Kayla Eggert; Product Development Specialist: Owen Hamlin

Statement on Usage of Generative Artificial Intelligence

Bearport Publishing remains committed to publishing high-quality nonfiction books. Therefore, we restrict the use of generative AI to ensure accuracy of all text and visual components pertaining to a book's subject. See BearportPublishing.com for details.

Quote Sources

Page 28: Emily Drabinski from "What's a book ban anyway? Depends on who you ask," *NPR*, June 10, 2024; Ed McBroom from "Senate Oversight Committee Takes Up Long-Awaited Legislation to Expand Freedom of Information Act to Governor, Legislature," *Michigan Senate Democrats*, Feb. 7, 2024; Sailaja Joshi from "There's a revolution happening in children's publishing–you can thank the book bans," *Fast Company*, April 4, 2024.

Library of Congress Cataloging-in-Publication Data is available at www.loc.gov or upon request from the publisher.

ISBN: 979-8-89232-761-9 (hardcover)
ISBN: 979-8-89232-938-5 (paperback)
ISBN: 979-8-89232-848-7 (ebook)

For more information, write to Bearport Publishing, 5357 Penn Avenue South, Minneapolis, MN 55419.

Contents

Access Denied

A library is filled with information. It has books and magazines. Many libraries have computers. Anyone who visits can **access** all this and more.

But what if someone decides a library shouldn't have certain books? Removing them is a kind of censorship.

Librarians usually pick books for their library. They try to have things for all readers. Different people want different kinds of books. Sometimes, people do not like the books meant for others.

Setting Limits

Censorship is limiting access. It can be done to ideas, images, words, or information.

Many types of things can be censored. A painting might be taken out of a museum. Or a book may be removed from a classroom. A song on streaming can have words cut out or changed.

Some styles of music are censored more. Blues, R&B, rap, and rock have been **challenged** the most. People may disagree with the words used. Sometimes, they say the topics of songs are not safe.

Some albums are sold with warning labels. The songs may be changed on streaming platforms.

Governments can censor things, too. They may make rules about what can be in the news. Or they could block social media. Sometimes, they **ban** certain books.

Anyone who breaks these rules can be punished. They may go to jail. In some cases, they are even killed.

Some governments use censorship to control their image. They ban negative stories. Even stories that are true may be blocked.

Why Censor?

People censor things for a few reasons. Often, they say it is to **protect** others. They warn words, topics, or images could harm people. Some think certain materials could give people dangerous information.

This is often said when people want to block violence. They believe seeing violence may make the viewers violent.

All governments keep some information from people. Details about parts of the military are secret. That is meant to keep soldiers safe. This usually isn't thought of as censorship.

Some people want to limit access to things for young people. Most people agree curse words are not good for kids. Many believe sex and sexuality are adult topics, too. They think these things should be censored.

Some adults don't want kids to learn about gender or sexual **identities**. They try to block things about lesbian, gay, bisexual, transgender, or queer (LGBTQ+) people.

Who Decides?

Some censorship is based on clear rules. There may be age limits on specific topics. But many times, decisions are based on personal beliefs. A small group may think something is wrong. Others may have different ideas. But everyone must live with the same rules.

In 1873, Congress made a law. It said people could not mail **offensive** materials. The law banned many things. It included a rule about the kinds of medical information doctors could mail.

NO!

It's Right

In the United States, speech is protected. It is part of the first **amendment** of the Constitution. The amendment says people cannot be stopped from saying what they want. This limits censorship.

However, it says only the government cannot stop speech. Individuals in private spaces can act differently.

The first amendment does not cover all speech. Lies in ads are not protected. Neither is knowingly telling lies about people. People also can't make threats of violence.

Speaking out at School

In the United States, many kinds of **protests** are legal, too. In 1965, students at one Iowa school protested the Vietnam War (1954–1975). They wore black armbands to class. The school suspended the students. But courts later decided students have the right to protest. Their views can't be censored.

In 2024, some college students protested against the Israel-Hamas war. Leaders of the schools stopped many of the protests. But the law says students have the right to speak.

Students have long led protest movements.

What's the Harm?

Even with protections, censorship still happens. Many think this can cause problems.

If information is censored, people cannot decide the truth. That may make it easy for people to cheat or lie. If politicians do this, it can harm the people they should be working for.

The Freedom of Information Act took effect in 1967. This law says people have the right to know what is happening in the government. They can ask to see government records.

President Lyndon Johnson signed the Freedom of Information Act into law.

When topics are censored in schools, students don't learn about them. However, this does not make the topics go away. Some say not knowing about historical violence can allow it to continue. They argue against censorship of **racism** and discrimination.

Many people think education should cover uncomfortable topics. They want students to learn to see all sides of an issue. They want to teach kids to discuss difficult things in a respectful way.

Today and Tomorrow

In recent years, censorship in schools has been big news. Across the country, people have been challenging some books. They think they are not okay for children. They want them taken out of libraries and classrooms.

However, others disagree. Librarians, teachers, parents, and students have spoken up.

In 2022, a Florida law said teachers could not talk about race or gender in school. Almost right away, people started fighting the law. They say it goes against the first amendment.

Students, parents, and teachers speak up at school board meetings.

The discussion about censorship will continue. Humans have always disagreed. People who want to censor things believe they are protecting others. Those who disagree believe access to information helps people learn and grow. There is no simple answer everyone can agree upon.

In the United Sates, everyone has the right to say what they think. People can ask to censor things. People can also fight against that censorship.

Voices in the News

People have many things to say about censorship. Some of their voices can be heard in the news.

Emily Drabinski
President of the American Library Association

"Many Americans . . . don't have access to books in any other way except through their library."

Ed McBroom
Michigan State Senator

"Having laws requiring openness of our government actions and records is a statement of our values in this government . . ."

Sailaja Joshi
Founder of Mango & Marigold Press

"The book bans just reinforce [kids'] sense of isolation and **marginalization**."

SilverTips for SUCCESS

★SilverTips for REVIEW

Review what you've learned. Use the text to help you.

Define key terms

access
ban
censor
first amendment
protest

Check for understanding

What is censorship? Give three examples of censorship.

Why might people want to censor something?

Explain one possible negative result of censorship.

Think deeper

Do you think information or art should ever be censored? Why or why not?

★SilverTips on TEST-TAKING

- **Make a study plan.** Ask your teacher what the test is going to cover. Then, set aside time to study a little bit every day.
- **Read all the questions carefully.** Be sure you know what is being asked.
- **Skip any questions** you don't know how to answer right away. Mark them and come back later if you have time.

Glossary

access the ability to see or get to something

amendment an official change made to the U.S. Constitution

ban to not allow people to see or do something

challenged questioned if something was right or not

identities the distinguishing characters and personalities of individuals

marginalization being placed in a powerless or limited position within a society or group

offensive able to cause upset or disgust

protect to keep safe from harm

protests demonstrations or public statements for or against things

racism the oppression of a racial group to the advantage of another

Read More

Bell, Samantha. *Freedom of Speech and the Press (Understanding American Democracy).* San Diego, CA: BrightPoint Press, 2024.

Jeffries, Joyce. *What's Censorship? (What's the Issue?).* Buffalo, NY: KidHaven Publishing, 2023.

Lyon, Jonah. *Pros and Cons: Banned Books (Two Sides of an Argument: Speech and Debate).* Ann Arbor, MI: Cherry Lake Publishing, 2023.

Learn More Online

1. Go to **FactSurfer.com** or scan the QR code below.
2. Enter "**Censorship**" into the search box.
3. Click on the cover of this book to see a list of websites.

Index

About the Author

Ashley Kuehl is an editor and writer specializing in nonfiction for young people. She lives in Minneapolis, MN.